Animals

Written by Lidia Kacelnik

Illustrated by Beccy Blake

MACMILLAN

Look! It's a giraffe.
It's tall. It's orange and brown.
It's enormous.

Wait a minute! There are one, two, three, four, five ladybugs. They're beautiful. They're red and black. They're tiny.

Is it an airplane? No, it isn't! It's a bird. It's an eagle. It's very strong.

This is an armadillo.
It's small. It eats ants.
Do you like ants? Yuck!

There's a crocodile in the river. It's green and gray. Its mouth is very big.

Look! It's a spider.
It's very hairy. Count the legs.
There are eight legs.

Oh look! There's a bird
and a flower. The bird is little.
It's green and blue.
The flower is purple.

This is a monkey. It lives in the jungle. It's brown and hairy. It eats bananas.

This is my home. It's in Antarctica. It's very cold. I like cold weather.
Antarctica

I live here with my family.
That's my mom, my dad, and
my little sister. We eat fish.
Yummy!

Here's a lion.
It's in Africa. It's big.
It's hungry.

There are hippos in the lake. There's a big hippo and a small hippo. What are they doing?

I don't believe it! It's an enormous cat. No, it isn't. It's a tiger!

Do you like elephants?
I like elephants. They're
enormous. They're gray and
they have big ears.

What's this? It's orange.
Let's see. It's yellow and black.
Oh no! Now it's green and
black. Oh! It changes color.
It's a chameleon.

What a surprise! It's a snake. I like snakes. This snake is yellow and black. Its body is long. It doesn't have any legs.

Look! My favorite animal is a hamster. She's my pet. Her name is Cathy.

Post-reading Activities

1 Solve the puzzle and write.

penguinolftdmonkeylowdehamsterflyugiraffejher

1  ____________

3  ____________

2  ____________

4  ____________

2 Read and color.

Penguin is black and white.
His hat is pink.
His backpack is blue
and green.
His hamster is brown.

3 Choose *true* or *false*.

1 Lions live in Antarctica.
true or *false*

2 A spider is black and hairy.
true or *false*

3 A giraffe is short.
true or *false*

4 Chameleons change color.
true or *false*

4 Make a tiger mask.

1 Draw a tiger's face.

2 Cut it out.

3 Color the tiger's face.

4 Punch two holes and put two pieces of string through.

5 Choose and color.

1 The giraffe is

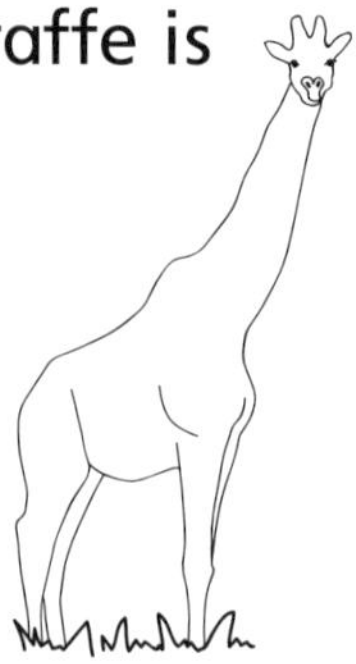

a blue and white.
b orange and brown.

2 The ladybugs are

a red and black.
b red and pink.

3 The bird is

a green and blue.
b green and yellow.

4 The snake is

a yellow and black.
b purple and black.

Answer Key

1 Solve the puzzle and write.

1 giraffe
2 hamster
3 monkey
4 penguin

2 Read and color.

3 Choose *true* or *false*.

1 false
2 true
3 false
4 true

4 Make a tiger mask.

5 Choose and color.

1 The giraffe is orange and brown.
2 The ladybugs are red and black.
3 The bird is green and blue.
4 The snake is yellow and black.

Macmillan Education
Between Towns Road, Oxford, OX4 3PP
A division of Macmillan Publishers Limited
Companies and representatives throughout the world

ISBN 1 405 00960 8

Written by Lidia Kacelnik

The author would like to thank Vale Noy for her editorial support.

Illustrated by Beccy Blake
Back cover illustration by Beccy Blake
Designed by Tamarillo Design
Cover photograph by Photodisc
Cover design by Tamarillo Design
Original cover concept by Phil Starr

The authors and publishers would like to thank the following for permission to reproduce the following photographic material:

Brand X Pictures p8; Corbis p13 ©Alissa Crandall; DigitalSTOCK pp2, 15; Digital Vision pp6, 16; Getty/Image Bank p3; John Foxx/Alamy/Imagestate pp9, 17; Photodisc pp4, 5, 7, 10, 12, 14.

Printed and bound in Thailand.

2008 2007 2006 2005
10 9 8 7 6 5 4 3